OUTDOOR COOKING

HEEL Verlag GmbH
Gut Pottscheidt
53639 Königswinter
Germany
Tel.: +49 2223 9230-0
Fax: +49 2223 9230-13
info@heel-verlag.de
www.heel-verlag.de

© 2020 HEEL Verlag GmbH, Königswinter, Germany
In Cooperation with Petromax

Author: Carsten Bothe
Design: HEEL Verlag GmbH, Axel Mertens
Editor: Ulrike Reihn-Hamburger

Photography:
Philipp Hympendahl, www.hympendahl.de
Assisted by: Daniel Koke
Except:
Sandra Then: 5 t, 5 m, 6, 11, 19, 21, 58/59, 61, 63, 65, 67, 68, 69, 73, 76,
98/99, 103, 105, 107, 110, 112/113, 115, 116/117, 120, 126/127, 128, 131,
132/133,
Fotolia.de: © mrstam (8), © Daxiao Productions (25 l), © Maksym Gorpenyuk
(50), © gameboyfoto (52 tr), © leelakajonkij (55 t), © losangela (82),
© Dani Vincek (83), © hans_chr (96), © bernardbodo (143 r),
© Petromax | Julia Reichardt/Christian Rößler/Jürgen Jeibmann
Photographik: 9, 12/13, 32, 41, 51, 56, 75, 125, 139, 140,
Indiana Andreae/Way Out Crew
(16 tl), Thorsten Brandenburg/BBQPit.de (124)
© Sascha Lotzmann, kuestenglut.de: 101

Printed in Poland

ISBN 978-3-95843-958-0

CARSTEN BOTHE

OUTDOOR COOKING

THE PETROMAX
COOKBOOK

HEEL

CONTENT

PREFACE

Dear Reader,

From the first spark on to blazing flames down to glowing embers—cooking outdoors in nature over the open fire exudes an unwavering fascination. Combined with a good pinch of adventure and originality there is more to it than mere food preparation. Thanks to the Petromax company, cooking and baking at the campfire and the "outdoor kitchen" has experienced an incredible boom over the past few years. However, for the outdoor kitchen not only excellent cast-iron equipment such as Dutch Ovens, Fire Skillets, Loaf Pans and Muffin Tins or other utensils is important, but one also needs reliable and workable recipes.

In this book, aside from classics such as Layered Meat or Cinnamon Rolls we also present some traditional recipes known as "poor man's food" or from the chuckwagon. Still, naturally, there are many news and numerous suggestions as well as field-tested tips on handling cast iron, fireplaces and co.

On that note I wish you a good time while cooking the recipes!

Yours,

Good food is
the foundation
of genuine
happiness.

(Georges Auguste Escoffier, 1846–1935,
French Chef)

WELCOME

Dear Reader,

No matter whether you are an outdoor cooking rookie or a professional campfire chef, what counts is that you live for Fire & Light, Grilling and Outdoor Cooking and may be also for Bushcraft & Survival. If so, we have something in common, because we at Petromax, the German traditional brand with the dragon, also live the passion for cooking outdoors. We need the aromatic smell of nature and the original campfire experience just as much as the air we breathe.

As premium supplier for high-quality and reliable cast and wrought-iron cookware as well as for further useful accessories we offer you coordinated and combinable tools for your cooking adventure. Dutch Ovens, Fire Skillets, Loaf Pans, Muffin Tin, Ring Cake Pan, Waffle Iron, compact barbecues and large camp kitchen: The Petromax product world has expanded the outdoor kitchen by many options. For any taste or requirement something perfectly suitable can be found.

With the Petromax Cookbook you hold in your hand a comprehensive collection of traditional but also newly interpreted dishes, a compendium for cooking, roasting, smoking and baking with and over the open fire. Cast iron can do anything is the slogan and you will be surprised about the diverse options with the hot iron. In addition to the recipes you can find all sorts of valuable information about handling and caring for cast iron and co. as well as some tips and tricks. Just as your equipment this cookbook is meant to accompany you for many years to come and serve you loyally when cooking outdoors.

We wish you much joy when cooking and trying out new dishes, always a crackling fire by your side and many intensive moments of adventure outdoors.

Jonas and Dr. Pia Christin Taureck

COOKING AND BAKING AT THE CAMPFIRE

Fresh bread or rolls, cinnamon rolls or a pie make the heart of campfire gourmets leap but only few dare to prepare such treats. Essentially, it is quite simple if you follow the recipes and approach the matter with a little skill and intuition. Practice makes perfect. First, try to prepare a pancake on the Fire Bowl, which is easy to make and makes you get used to handling the batter.

When trying the recipes for the first time we suggest that you stick to the recipe. Start off with simple recipes and vary as little ingredients as possible. As soon as you have followed a recipe several times with a satisfying result, you can start to alter the recipe by varying only one ingredient at a time.

COOKING AND BAKING TIMES

The cooking and baking times basically depend on the energy that emits from the charcoal. However, in general, the following applies: Start in good time and finish cooking the food first and keep it warm afterwards. This is better than being tempted to raise the cooking temperature.

As a standard value keep in mind: The first kilogram of meat needs about 1 hour to cook. The second kilogram needs another 45 minutes and any further kilogram another additional 30 minutes. A roast of three kilograms would thus need about 2 hours and 15 minutes.

For certainty, use an inserting thermometer. While inserting, pay close attention to the feeling you have: Do you feel muscle fibres or does the needle just sink in easily? The meat should not only reach a certain temperature, but also be soft.

KEY

 Skillets

 Loaf Pan

 Ring Cake Pan

 Griddle and Fire Bowl

 Muffin Tin

 Cooking Tripod

 Dutch Oven

 Campfire Skewers

 Waffle Iron

 Sandwich Iron

 Pyron Plate

 Burger Iron

 Teakettle

half ring = low heat

whole ring = medium heat

THE SIMPLE RING METHOD FOR HEAT CONTROL

When heating up the Dutch Oven, you will have some questions according to the number of briquettes, cooking temperatures etc. Needless to say, you wish for specific instructions but there are too many variables to consider, such as weather, charcoal type, outer temperatures, etc. However, to simplify matters: There are only three different settings, namely low heat, medium heat and strong heat.

Form a tight ring of charcoal at the edge of the lid as well as below the pot. As the pot diameter is less at the bottom, there will be less charcoal as on top of the lid. This is the starting point for medium heat. However, the charcoal shall not remain in the initial position but is to be distributed evenly on the lid and below the pot. The ring is only formed to calculate the amount of charcoal. For low heat, remove every second piece of charcoal from the ring. For strong heat, put as many pieces of charcoal onto the lid and below the pot as possible.

OVEN TEMPERATURES

If you want to prepare a dish in your oven at home instead of the fire, please select the following temperatures:

one and a half ring = strong heat

Half ring 180 °C, whole ring: 200 °C
One and a half ring: 220 °C
This is not the temperature within the Dutch Oven but the setting temperature of your baking oven! If possible, choose convection and, if not, top and bottom heat work fine as well.

AMERICAN BREAKFAST

The American breakfast with bacon, eggs, sausages, baked beans and pancakes is prepared in no time at all. But be aware! The smell of roasted bacon will attract people from all around.

The bacon is laid flat into a cold, dry pan. Heat up the pan until the bacon dries up and turns golden brown. Turn the bacon and roast from the other side.
Now, there is room in the pan to roast the Nuremberg sausages. Simply put them next to the bacon and roast from both sides.
Take the bacon out of the pan and place it on a paper cloth to let the oil drain. Crack one or two eggs per person into the pan and cook as desired. Take the sausages and eggs out of the pan and put aside.
To prepare the pancakes, mix the egg, milk and oil. Add the dry ingredients little by little, mix to a thick batter and let it rest for some minutes. Bake the pancakes in the pan, with some butter.

Finally, heat up the baked beans in the hot pan.

INGREDIENTS FOR THE PANCAKES PER SERVING:

1 cup flour

2 tbsp. sugar

1 tsp. baking soda

1 tsp. baking powder

1 trace salt

1 egg

200 ml milk

3 tbsp. oil

AS DESIRED:

bacon

sausages

eggs

beans

Do serve maple syrup with the pancakes!

BACON AND EGGS

Everyone knows bacon and eggs from home, but my special recipe is undeniably tasty: Roast the bacon dice in some butter until crispy, add diced onions and roast until translucent. Finally, crack the eggs on top and only stir a little. There should be yellow and white spots and no evenly distributed mass. The dish tastes best with pepper and chive rolls sprinkled on top, directly from pan with a buttered slice of bread or a roll.

German farmer's breakfast

GERMAN FARMER'S BREAKFAST

A full German farmer's breakfast is the best start into your day, when planning to go hiking or doing any other physically challenging tour. It is also perfectly appropriate as a fast lunch. The base makes boiled jacket potatoes (or simply boiled potatoes) from the previous day. It is served with a slice of buttered rye bread, a pickle and a dash of Maggi seasoning. As it is a typical bachelor's meal, the amount of ingredients depends on your hunger.

INGREDIENTS PER SERVING:

1-2 large boiled potatoes

½ onion

½ cup bacon dice (or sausage dice)

1-2 eggs

1 pickle

pepper and salt

chive

clarified butter for roasting

Cut the cold potatoes into slices or dice and roast in a large pan with abundant clarified butter. When the potatoes turn brown, add the bacon dice. When the bacon becomes crisp, add the onion dice and roast until translucent. Crack the eggs on top, stir and let thicken. If using a cast-iron pan, you can already take it from the fire, as the residual heat is sufficient. Season to taste with pepper. Taste before adding salt, as the bacon already is salty.
Serve on a plate with a pickle on the side and with chive rolls on top.

EGGS BENEDICT

This traditional American breakfast is a more refined version of the farmer's breakfast. The freshly poached eggs are perfect for a cosy breakfast for two.

INGREDIENTS PER SERVING:

2 fresh eggs

1 slice of bread or 1 roll

1 slice of cooked ham or bacon

2 egg yolks

1 tbsp. lemon juice

1 tbsp. crème fraiche

1 tsp. sugar

150 g butter

pepper and salt

chive and parsley as garnish

Crack the eggs into a cup, without breaking the yolks. Let salted water with a dash of vinegar boil in a large pot suspended on a Cooking Tripod. Hang the pot somewhat higher to prevent the water from continuously boiling. Use a whisk to generate a water whirl inside the pot. Carefully pour the eggs from a low height into the centre of the whirl.
The water must be moving to ensure that the eggs remain intact. Let cook for 2 to 3 minutes, then take out the eggs and let dry on a paper cloth.
At the same time, roast the ham or bacon in a pan, toast the bread or roll halves and spread with butter.
To prepare the hollandaise sauce, whisk the egg yolks with lemon juice, some salt, sugar and crème fraiche. Briefly boil the butter and add slowly, while whisking vigorously. Season with salt and pepper.
Place the ham onto the bread, add the eggs and top it off with hollandaise sauce. Garnish with some chive or parsley and serve immediately.

CHEESE BALLS

INGREDIENTS:

100 g Brie, 70 % FiDM

100 g Romadur

½ tbsp. soft cheese

1 onion

½ tsp. chilli powder

1 pinch salt

1 pinch freshly ground pepper

breadcrumbs

fat for frying

Peel the onion and cut with the cheese into coarse dice. Blend both and season with chilli, salt and pepper. Add sufficient breadcrumbs for a smooth dough.

With damp hands, form small balls and roll in breadcrumbs. Place the prepared cheese balls in the freezer for 1-2 hours.

Briefly fry the cheese balls in boiling oil in the Dutch Oven. The crust should be crispy brown. Use a skimmer to take out the cheese balls and let fat drain onto a paper cloth. Serve with a sauce to your liking.

Cheese balls

EMPANADAS

Empanadas are fried dumplings, filled with meat and vegetables, that are served in almost every Tapas bar in Spain. Originally, it is a poor man's dish to use up leftovers from the previous day.

INGREDIENTS FOR 25 PIECES

Pizza dough from 500 g flour (see page 111)

500 g pulled pork (approx. 1 tbsp. per dumpling)

roasted onions

sauerkraut

Prepare a simple pizza dough and roll it out to knife thickness. Use a glass or cup (not too small) to cut out circles. Put one tablespoon of pulled pork (or other kind of meat) and a portion of topping on top. Coleslaw is not as suitable as pre-cooked types, such as onions or Sauerkraut. The meat should be finely cut. To facilitate handling, fold down the dough slightly over edge, spread yolk or water on the edge and press down the edge with a fork, to generate the typical pattern. The empanadas are fried in fat (or olive oil, as in Spain) and placed onto a paper cloth to drain oil. Empanadas are a typical finger food that is, due to size, eaten with only two bites.

You can also prepare larger empanadas of 15 cm in diameter, two of which are then served on one plate per person. These would not be fried but coated with egg yolk and baked in the oven, on the Pyron Plate, the grill or in the Dutch Oven.

FRENCH TOAST

When having children around, you will never go wrong with French toast.

INGREDIENTS PER SERVING:

1 stale toast

1 egg

2 tbsp. cream or evaporated milk

sugar and cinnamon

maple syrup and/or apple sauce,

some butter as desired

Remove the crust of the toast. Whisk the egg with some cream or condensed milk and soak the bread. Bake in plenty of butter and serve with sugar and cinnamon, maple syrup or apple sauce.

The left-over bread crust can be used for burger patties.

French toast

Empanadas

STIR FRY RECIPES

Gyro is prepared easily and hardly requires any tableware especially when served in pita bread.

INGREDIENTS FOR 4 SERVINGS:

1 kg pork (cutlet or fillet)

5 onions

5 tbsp. oil

2 garlic cloves

1 tbsp. gyro seasoning

1 tbsp. paprika

1 tsp. curry

pita bread

PAN GYRO

Cut the meat in gyro-typical stripes. Cut the onions in rings and put some rings aside as garnish. Cover the meat with the spices and the pressed garlic, pour oil on top and let soak for at least one hour at a cool place, even better over night. After marinating the gyro meat, sear it in a pan. The gyro is served with Zaziki, coleslaw or rice, topped with onion rings and parsley. You can cut open half a pita bread, put inside coleslaw and gyro and top it off with Zaziki and onion rings.

TYROLESE GRÖSTL

Cut the cooked beef into thin slices and roast to brown on the outside and still juicy inside. Peel and slice the cold potatoes. Add the potatoes to the meat and let brown on one side. Turn them and add the onions. Cook everything until the onions become translucent. Season to your liking with pepper, salt, marjoram and caraway. Before serving, sprinkle with chopped parsley or chive. Then place the pan with the Gröstl on the table.

Additionally, when cooking beef, you receive a savoury stock.

The Tyrolese Gröstl is a typical dish to use up leftovers and is unbelievably tasty. As every alp has a large pan used to prepare various pastries, this pan is also used to prepare the Gröstl.

INGREDIENTS FOR 4 SERVINGS:

500 g cooked beef

1 kg jacket potatoes

1 large onion

lard for roasting

pepper and salt

marjoram, dried

caraways, ground

fresh parsley or chive, to sprinkle

SCHNITZEL

Cold Schnitzels always are a welcome snack in-between meals, for picnics or in a roll as a second breakfast.

INGREDIENTS PER SERVING:

300 g Schnitzel meat (ham or back)

eggs, for coating

flour

breadcrumbs

pepper and salt

clarified butter for roasting

To roast a good Schnitzel is fairly easy but the workspace, especially with limited resources, should be well and cleanly prepared. First, pound the meat until evenly flat. When on the way, this can be done using a pot with handle or a pan.

Next, prepare the battering line that ends right next to the pan, to prevent making a mess on the entire table. The first plate is the one with the pound meat. The next one is covered with flour, then follows one with whisked eggs and, finally, there is the plate with breadcrumbs right next to the pan.

Heat up the pan with abundant clarified butter. Take the first Schnitzel and cover entirely with flour. Dip into the eggs and then into the breadcrumbs. Place in the pan and repeat the process for all the other Schnitzel.

Roast the Schnitzel from both sides until golden brown. Serve right away or let cool to be eaten at a later time.

POTATO PANCAKES

The typical aspect of roasting potato pancakes is the lingering smell of fat in the flat. This is not an issue while camping and cooking outdoors on a grill or mobile cooker.

INGREDIENTS PER SERVING:

1 large potato

1 egg

1 small onion

1 tbsp. flour

pepper and salt

Grate the raw, peeled potatoes and onions. Let the mass rest for some time and drain the water that gathers in the bottom of the bowl. Add the eggs, pepper and salt and the flour.

Heat up some lard or clarified butter in the pan and roast the potato pancakes from both sides until golden brown and crisp.

Potato pancakes

VEGETABLES ON THE GRIDDLE AND FIRE BOWL

There are some types of vegetables that cannot be prepared directly in the embers and are better prepared on a hot Griddle and Fire Bowl. These are, among others, tomatoes and leek.

TOMATOES

For this dish, you need very ripe and aromatic tomatoes. They contain sugar that shall caramelise in a dry pan or griddle. The tomatoes should be no larger than golf-ball size.

Cut the tomatoes in halves and put the cut side onto the hot Griddle and Fire Bowl or a dry pan. The tomatoes will and shall stick on immediately. After a while, they will become soft and collapse slightly. Use a spatula to scrape them off and, turned over, put them on a plate. Add some pepper, salt and high-quality olive oil, or even better garlic oil. That's the taste of a perfectly grilled tomato!

LEEK

When cooked to softness, the thick leek sticks are a true delicacy and a nice alternative side dish for a BBQ. You need at least one leek stick per person, the hot Griddle and Fire Bowl and a newspaper.

Cut off the roots, to be able to eat the leek right after cooking. Also cut the green, dry top part you do not want to eat. Some people like their leek green, others white. It is important to remove the sand as best as possible, without cutting the leek open. Washing and shaking should be sufficient.

Put the leek onto the hot Griddle and Fire Bowl and leave until completely black. Turn the leek to blacken on all sides. Take the sticks from the fire and wrap them in some layers of newspaper. Let the wrapped leek rest for well 15 minutes next to the fire. A thermo box can come in handy. During this time, the heat of the outer leaves will soften the inner part of the leek and the sticks will become tender.

Unwrap the leek and remove the blackened outer leaves, to enjoy the soft, delicious inside. Some butter and salt is all it takes!

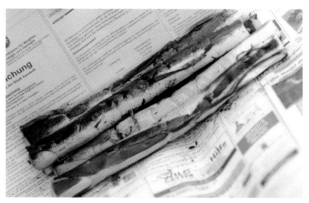

SPAGHETTI CARBONARA

One calculates about 150-200 g spaghetti per person which means that one 500 g pack usually suffices for three people. The pasta can be cooked a day in advance to take them along pre-cooked on the camping trip. For that purpose, they must be rinsed immediately after cooking and topped with some oil, so they won't stick together.

Let the spaghetti cook in a pot with salted water until al dente.

In a pan, roast the diced bacon and the onions until translucent. Add the spaghetti to the pan.

In a bowl, mix the egg, cream and parmesan and season with salt and pepper. Pour the mass over the spaghetti and let thicken while stirring.

INGREDIENTS PER SERVING:

150-200 g spaghetti

1 egg

½ cup cream

1 tbsp. ground parmesan

½ cup diced bacon

½ onion

pepper and salt

MEAT, FISH, POULTRY

TROUT

Trouts are an excellent food fish and available everywhere—if not fresh then at least frozen.

For one person the calculated amount is about 350-380 g (ready to cook with head). For grilling or roasting in a pan the fish should be no larger than 500 g otherwise the muscle parts are uneven and the tail would overcook while the neck would still be glassy. Larger fish are filleted and roasted in smaller parts. Basically, the trout is cleaned, acidulated with lemon juice and salted. Further preparation depends on the recipe.

TROUT MILLER STYLE

The clean, acidulated and salted trout is entirely covered in abundant flour. Roast the fish for 5 minutes from each side.
Serve with green salad and parsley potatoes as well as horseradish cream.

TROUT GARDEN STYLE

Fill the trout with abundant garden herbs as well as freshly cut garlic and roast it swimming on butter, also adding the cut garlic and herbs to the pan.

TROUT WITH ALMOND BUTTER

Keep the trout "miller style" warm, melt one teaspoon of butter in the pan and add a tablespoon of almond flakes. When golden brown, pour the butter and almonds over the trout.
A fresh cucumber salad is the perfect side dish.

OPTION

Instead of trout, use a fresh mackerel or for the true fish fan a green herring.

Use the spatula or spoon to skim fat from the pan and pour it onto the trout, especially over the tail if protruding at the edge of the pan.

LAYERED MEAT

Season the pork slices with steak seasoning and cut the onions in 5 mm thick slices.

Place the Dutch Oven on its side and tightly stack the ingredients in alternation, having the meat in upright position when turning the Dutch Oven upright again. At the end, pour a cup of ketchup or steak sauce on top, which will be the only fluid you add and the rest will be meat juice or juice from the onions.

Put a few glowing charcoals below the pot and on top of the lid and let the meat cook for about 2 hours until the first pieces turn brown.

Layered meat is a true Dutch Oven classic. The dish not only is very easy to prepare but can also be varied with herbs and steak sauces.

FOR 6-8 SERVINGS IN FT6 OR FT9

2.5 kg pork neck, cut in slices

steak seasoning

2-3 large Spanish onions

15 slices smoked bacon; 3-4 mm thick

1 cup steak sauce to your liking or smoked ketchup

Only use BBQ spices cautiously, as a lot of them contain a high amount of salt which will spoil the dish, especially with bacon as ingredient. Rather prepare your own BBQ spice with less or no salt at all.

35

HAMBURGER/ CHEESEBURGER

The true king of fast food!

THE MEAT
A real hamburger patty is solely made of beef and fat. The raw patty should be a little larger than the bun, as it shrinks slightly when grilled. If you make an indentation in the middle of the patty, it will not bulge during roasting but stay nicely flat. According to taste you can add various cheeses or vegetables.

THE BUN
Not only a burger bun is a suitable roll. If you do not overdo the filling a bread roll with crispy crust can be a nice alternative, or you choose pita bread cut into quarters. Before filling, roast the cut edges so that the bread has more "standing".

THE CHEESE
Be creative when choosing the cheese and take something different than the trusty orange-yellow Cheddar. Roquefort, Greyerzer or a piece of Gouda from the kitchen table will give your hamburger a whole new flavour. Put the cheese directly onto the hot meat to have it melt.

TOMATO
Cut a large beef tomato in thin slices. This will make it much easier to eat the burger than with small tomato slices falling out of the bun.

ONIONS
Take a large onion and cut it into thin slices. For that purpose, a vegetable slicer is a useful tool. You can add the onions raw or roasted and translucent to your burger, just as you prefer. You can even cook the onions to a jam, as described on page 82.

CUCUMBERS
A real burger also requires some slices of cucumber. Still, not everyone likes them pickled with vinegar or salt. Cucumbers will also do just fine.

SALAD
Basically, any type of salad can be used but iceberg lettuce has a deliciously crispy structure.

BACON
Two to three slices of bacon are roasted on the grill and added to the burger. Make sure that the bacon does not lose too much fat when dripping into the embers and thus causing uprising flames on the grill.

SAUCES
Ketchup is a must but also a good steak sauce is welcome. Additionally, use mayonnaise or a special burger sauce. Spread the light sauce on the upper bun half and the red sauce on the lower half.

Alternatively, you can also roast the patties in the Burger Iron.

BAVARIAN MEAT LOAF WITH FRIED EGG IN A ROLL

A typical "Bavarian hamburger."

INGREDIENTS PER SERVING:

1 pretzel roll

1 slice Bavarian meat loaf, thick as a finger

1 egg

sweet mustard

iceberg lettuce

some pickles

½ onion

butter

Roast the Bavarian meat loaf slice from both sides and, next to it, fry an egg "over well" to prevent the yolk from spilling out of the burger. Cut the pretzel in halves and roast the cut surface. Spread butter on the lower half, then put a lettuce leaf on top, add the meat slice, the fried egg, some onion rings and, finally, some sliced pickles and spread sweet mustard on the upper pretzel half before closing the burger.

Without tarragon and mustard, the Bearnaise sauce will be a great Hollandaise sauce.

This is a perfect group dish, as it is prepared in a large pan and can easily be stretched if there are more guests than expected after all.

INGREDIENTS PER SERVING:

300 g pork fillet

1 small onion

5 fresh mushrooms

½ tsp. green, pickled pepper, without brine

FOR SAUCE BEARNAISE:

2 egg yolks

1 tbsp. lemon juice

1 tsp. tarragon, dried

1 tsp. Dijon mustard

1 tbsp. crème fraiche

1 tsp. sugar

150 g butter

pepper and salt

FILLET BEARNAISE

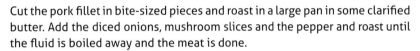

Cut the pork fillet in bite-sized pieces and roast in a large pan in some clarified butter. Add the diced onions, mushroom slices and the pepper and roast until the fluid is boiled away and the meat is done.

For the sauce, whisk the yolk with lemon juice, tarragon, mustard, some salt, sugar and crème fraiche. Shortly boil up the butter and slowly add to the mass, while whisking vigorously. Season with salt and pepper.

Deglaze the meat with the sauce and may be add some water for the right consistency. Without tarragon and mustard, the Bearnaise sauce will be a great Hollandaise sauce.

Serve with fresh white bread, potato wedges or potatoe rösti.

Pork fillet flambé

A traditional dish that—thanks to its few ingredients and cooking tools—is ideal for outdoor cooking and camping.

INGREDIENTS:

300 g liver slices

1 large onion

2-3 apple slices (Boskoop)

flour for dusting

milk or buttermilk to marinate

clarified butter

LIVER BERLIN STYLE

Cut the liver into slices and let them marinate in milk or buttermilk for some hours. If you like the typical liver taste you can skip that step. Afterwards, dry the liver and roll in some flour. Roast the liver in some clarified butter and, finally, add the apple slices and onion rings.

To finish, generously season with salt and pepper and serve with apple slices and onion rings. For people preferring a sweet component it can be served with cranberry jam. Serve with mashed potatoes.

This recipe is also well suited for beef fillet or game fillet.

PORK FILLET FLAMBÉ

As show element during cooking, a flambé makes a big impression! A flambé should be done in the dark, as the blue flame of the burning alcohol is hardly visible otherwise. Only use a small pan, such as the Wrought-Iron pan sp24, to have enough time to flip the individual pieces of meat. In a large pan, you have the risk of burned meat. Caution! Only pour alcohol from a glass and never from the bottle, as it might explode!

Remove the tendons from the pork fillets and cut in thumb-thick slices. Salt and pepper from both sides and heat up the wrought-iron pan. With its longer handle it is easier to handle.

Roast the pieces from both sides until almost done, still being slightly pink on the inside. Sauté the finely chopped shallot or onion and add the spirit from the glass. At the open fire, it will immediately ignite or, if not, slightly tilt the pan. Let the alcohol burn down and add wine to your taste and, finally, a good dash of cream.

INGREDIENTS:

250-300 g pork fillet, per person

1 shallot

1 glass schnapps

1 tbsp. wine

3 tbsp. cream (or evaporated milk)

Roulades are a classic German home cooked meal which has sadly been neglected for some time. They are easy to prepare, and a Dutch Oven is the perfect tool for that purpose.

First, you need large, thinly cut slices of meat from the topside. An artist is able to cut freehand with a large knife but most butchers use a cutting machine.

There are two options for filling: You either fill the meat with the ingredients as a whole, if you have very large slices, or you dice the ingredients and cover the meat slices with it, which is the way to go for smaller slices. Afterwards, roll up the roulades and secure them with a roulade needle or some thread. As soon as they are roasted they will hold on their own.

INGREDIENTS:

1-2 roulades, per person

tomato purée

root vegetables, if desired

stock or gravy

some cream (or sauce thickener)

PER ROULADE:

1 tbsp. mustard

¼ pickle

½ small onion

1-2 bacon slices

pepper, salt and paprika

some sugar

ROULADES

Place the beef roulade on a cutting board and spread mustard on top, then salt and pepper. Put the bacon and some onion rings lengthwise onto the roulade. Now, put the quartered pickle lengthwise at the short edge of the meat slice, roll up the roulade and secure with thread. You can prepare and roast the roulades one day in advance and finish cooking them the next day. That way you do not need to start cooking so early, as the time-consuming preparation is already done.

The rolled-up roulades are roasted dark on all sides in some fat inside the lid of the Dutch Oven. Use as many charcoals as you can fit below the lid. Put the roulades aside after roasting.

Roast a tablespoon of tomato purée, add abundant pepper, salt and paprika and if you like the remaining onions and root vegetables. Add some stock or, even better, gravy and stir to dissolve the roasting residues. Put the roulades back into the sauce. They should be covered at least by half. The cooking time is at least 2 hours, better 3 hours. During cooking, turn the roulades from time to time and check if the meat is already tender. Use only 10 charcoals, as the pot should only simmer. There are no charcoals needed on the lid.

Before serving, thicken the sauce with some cream or thickener.

You can prepare smaller roulades by finely dicing the onions, pickles and bacon and before rolling spreading it onto the meat like a filling.

You can also stack the roulades into two layers into a deep Dutch Oven. Make sure to have enough sauce and to restack the roulades from top to bottom every hour. You can also stack the roulades on Stack Grates inside the Dutch Oven, which will save you the restacking.

PORK ROAST À LA ROTISSERIE

This is an easy recipe with undeniably delicious results. When shopping the ingredients, make sure that the meat will fit into your Dutch Oven.

INGREDIENTS:

1 neck of pork, boneless (approx. 300-400 g pp)

onions (500 g per kg meat)

rotisserie roast seasoning

olive oil

The meat should weigh no more than 3 kg to be cooked in the Dutch Oven. A larger roast should be separated and prepared simultaneously in several Dutch Ovens.

Mix the oil with the seasoning until a thin paste develops. Cut the onions in coarse rings and fold in. Coat the pork with the paste. For a very thick roast, cut it lengthwise to allow the seasoning to penetrate into the meat. Put the roast with the remaining paste in a zipper bag or a glass bowl, mix well and let it marinate in the refrigerator or another cool place for one day. Restack every 4-6 hours to redistribute the oil.

Remove the onions from the roast—onions caught in a cut can be left—and sear the meat from both sides in the hot Dutch Oven. Oil is not required, as the meat still contains sufficient oil from marinating. Afterwards, add the onion oil seasoning paste and roast. Add one cup of water per kilogram of meat to prevent it from burning, then close the lid with charcoals on top.

The first kilogram of meat needs approx. 1 hour of cooking. The second kilogram requires further 45 minutes and each other kilogram additional 30 minutes. Thus, a roast of 3 kg needs about 2 hours and 15 minutes to cook.

Side dishes: Sauce with stewed onions, rye rolls and coleslaw.

PORK ROAST WITH CRACKLING

A roast with crackling is ideal when intially starting to cook with the Dutch Oven. It is a readily cured pork ham which is available at a relatively low price at the butcher or the wholesale market.

INGREDIENTS:

1 roast with crackling from the silverside, cured

2 onions

rye rolls

Use a sharp knife to cut the rind down to the meat and season with pepper. Place inside a suitable Dutch Oven, add quartered onions, some pepper and a cup of water. It is not necessary to roast the meat in advance.

Let cook for 2 hours at very low top heat until the roast is done. Afterwards, put fresh embers onto the lid. The top heat will make the crust nicely brown and crispy.

Three kilograms of meat require a little more than two hours of cooking. Serve the roast cut open, in a fresh rye roll.

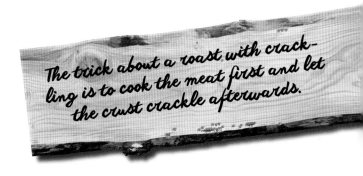

The trick about a roast with crackling is to cook the meat first and let the crust crackle afterwards.

Pork roast
with crackling

A pie can be filled in various ways either with a sweet or fruity stuffing or with a savoury one. Usually meat stuffings contain fillets or liver. Pies are mostly eaten cold and can be stored for several days. For a meat pie it helps to pour aspic into the crust, as the stuffing will shrink and peel from the crust.

FOR THE DOUGH:

700 g flour

150 g butter

1 egg

1 cup cold water

1 tsp. salt

FOR THE STUFFING:

500 g fat minced pork, preferably minced two times

5 large, coarse, raw sausages with the casing removed

100 g mushrooms

1 onion

1 glass red wine

herbs to taste

pepper and salt

1 egg yolk

MEAT PIE

Pour the flour into a bowl and add the cold, diced butter as well as salt. Knead butter and flour until it has a grit-like consistency. Now, add the egg and, little by little, add cold water until the dough is an elastic mass. Cover the dough and let it rest for at least half an hour. Roll out ¾ of the dough and cut into fitting pieces to line the baking pan. Flatten the remaining quarter of dough to cover the stuffing. Due to consistency, there will be about one third offcuts when cutting the dough. These can be used to garnish the pie.

For the stuffing, roast finely chopped onions and mushrooms in some fat. Mix both with red wine and chopped herbs and some salt and pepper as well as the minced meat. Knead the mixture well and firmly fill it into the pan lined with dough, leaving one finger's width of dough protruding. Cover the pie with the pre-formed dough lid and press the edges together to seal the pie. Use a sharp knife to cut a hole of approx. 1-Euro-coin size into the dough lid and stick a "chimney" of aluminium foil inside. To have it brown nicely, coat the pie with some yolk. Close the lid of the pan and bake the pie at medium top and bottom heat until it reaches at least 80 °C on the inside and the dough lid is turning golden brown. This will take about 1 ½ hours. It is sufficient to only put charcoal besides the baking pan and a few on the lid. Let the pie cool down inside the mould and, to serve, cut in semi-thick slices.

When preparing the pie with lid outdoors on the fire it should not rise higher than to one finger's width below the edge. When cooking it at home without lid, the baking pan can be filled higher.

The German meat loaf is traditionally filled with boiled eggs.

INGREDIENTS:

1 kg mixed, minced meat

3 eggs

2 stale rolls

milk

2 tbsp. mustard

stock

pepper and salt

2 onions for the sauce

sauce thickener, flour or cream

GERMAN MEAT LOAF

Soak the rolls in some milk and squeeze out the excess. Place the minced meat, the rolls and mustard in a bowl and generously season with salt and pepper. Knead well until forming a homogeneous mass.

Form a long loaf, cut it open lengthwise at the bottom and try to place three hard boiled, peeled eggs as centrally as possible inside and close the loaf again.

Sear the loaf in hot fat from all sides and add some coarsely cut onions to roast alongside. Add some water or stock and let the loaf cook for about 1 ½ hours. Take it out of the Dutch Oven and serve it on the lid, together with green beans or peas. Add some thickener, flour or cream to thicken the sauce and serve with boiled or mashed potatoes.

This meat loaf is an everyday dish in the USA. It is prepared with varying ingredients and every family has its own recipe. You can add various spices, such as chopped jalapeños. Maize grains or bell pepper dice also make a nice change.

FOR THE LOAF:

500 g minced meat

2 eggs

1-2 stale rolls

200 ml milk

1 onion, finely chopped

fresh parsley, chopped

1 tsp. oregano, dried

pepper and salt

FOR THE GLAZE:

¼ cup ketchup

1 tsp. mustard

½ tsp. nutmeg

1 tbsp. brown sugar

1 splash tabasco

1 tbsp. lemon juice

AMERICAN MEAT LOAF

For the glaze mix the ingredients well until the sugar has dissolved and spread the mixture onto the meat loaf, before baking.

Let the rolls soak in a bowl of milk. Take them out and squeeze out the excess. Pour the minced meat and the other ingredients into a large bowl and knead well until they form a homogeneous mass. Grease the Loaf Pan and fill in the mass, cover the surface with the sauce and put sufficient blazing charcoal below the pan and on top of the lid.
After 30 minutes, check if the loaf is done, with a core temperature of above 75 °C and the escaping fluid being clear.

Before taking it out and cutting it, let the loaf rest for 10 minutes inside the pan. For a picnic, keep the loaf inside the pan and cut it when on site. Mashed potatoes and vegetables are suitable side dishes.

A wonderful dish with a twist of flavour. This dish is traditionally eaten with maize porridge (a type of polenta) made from maize flour, but rice also works well.

INGREDIENTS FOR 6-8 SERVINGS IN FT9 OR FT12:

1 chicken, approx. 1.4 kg
(or chicken legs)

3 big onions

2 garlic cloves

2 carrots

1 small kohlrabi

1 aubergine

250 g mushrooms

½ celery root

1-2 leeks

2 bell peppers

800 ml coconut milk

1 tin pineapple with juice

pepper and salt

3 tbsp. curry

sambal oelek or harissa

If possible:
fresh ginger or lemon grass

CHICKEN CURRY

Cut the chicken into small pieces, the vegetable into small dice and the leek into rings. The trick is to cut up the vegetables into differently sized pieces to prevent them from collapsing into a mass. Pieces of match head size: celery, ginger, garlic. Pieces of cherry size: eggplant, turnip, mushrooms. Cut the bell pepper into pieces the size of about 1 Euro coin. Cut the onions in eighth, having pieces instead of rings. Cut the carrots into very thin slices or, even better, into thin strips.

Strongly heat up a Dutch Oven with pieces of thumb-thick wood. Have one bowl with the cut ingredients and an empty one ready for the roasted ones. Pour half a cup of oil into the pot and roast the chicken in portions, until nicely brown. Take it out by means of a skimmer and put aside in the empty bowl. One after one, roast all chicken parts and dust with curry powder, when in the bowl. Do not cut the lemon grass, as it cannot be eaten. Only knot together to facilitate taking it out after cooking.

Little by little, roast the vegetables and also put aside in the bowl. Add some oil if needed.
When everything is roasted, add the pineapple and coconut milk along with all roasted ingredients to the pot and stir cautiously. Season to your taste with harissa or sambal oelek, salt and pepper. The fluid should only just cover the vegetables.

Now, let simmer for two hours heated with little embers or only the radiating heat from the fire. The heat of burning wood, as used for roasting, would be too high and the dish would inevitably burn.

INGREDIENTS FOR ABOUT 30 PIECES:

500 g chicken breast

FOR THE MARINADE:

1 small piece fresh ginger

½ cup coconut milk

4 tbsp. light soy sauce

½ tsp. sambal oelek

1 tsp. coriander, ground

2 tsp. brown sugar

salt

FOR THE SAUCE:

1 small piece fresh ginger

100 g chunky peanut butter

250 ml coconut milk

1 tsp. sambal oelek

2 tsp. brown sugar

2 tbsp. lime juice

salt

SATAY SKEWERS

These skewers are a perfect finger food or served as main dish with rice.

Cut the meat into long, thin stripes and water the wood sticks.
Mix the finely grated ginger with the coconut milk, the soy sauce, sambal oelek, coriander, sugar and salt to a marinade. Let the meat soak in this marinade for some hours or over night at a cool place.

Slowly boil up the peanut butter, finely grated ginger, coconut milk, sambal oelek and sugar in a pot. The sauce should cook until creamy and is, then, seasoned with salt and lime juice.

Skewer the meat in waves onto the wood sticks and roast from all sides, for some minutes. Serve it hot together with the sauce.

DUCK WITH RED CABBAGE

Red cabbage is an excellent side dish for duck. When cooking a duck of about 2.4 kg the Dutch Ovens ft6 or ft9 are the perfect choice. Cooked on a bed of red cabbage, the duck will be wonderfully soft. It will have no crispy crust, which is of minor importance with the meat having an excellent flavour.

INGREDIENTS:

1 duck (approx. 2.4 kg)

800 ml red cabbage, from a can

2 small or 1 large apple (e.g. Boskoop)

2 onions

small potatoes, waxy

pepper and salt

Cut the duck open at the back and season with salt and pepper. Pour the red cabbage, the diced onions and diced apples into the Dutch Oven. The duck is placed on top with its breast facing upwards. Let cook for one hour, then check if there is still sufficient fluid. Afterwards, the duck is cooked for at least another half hour. The duck is done when the meat strips off the bone, which can take up to 2 ½ hours. In the meantime, the red cabbage is cooked within the meat juice making it incomparably delicious.

One hour before the cooking time is up, place small, peeled, waxy potatoes around the duck, to have another side dish ready at once.

Satay skewers

Quails are a nice starter and also a delicious main course. They taste especially good on a mixed meat platter served with couscous. The quails are filled with one date and one shallot each, supporting the wonderful taste. Frozen quails are always available and regarding the price per kilogram they are not much more expensive than duck.

Couscous is an excellent side dish for campfire cooking as it only needs to be poured over with hot water. Let well for several minutes by the campfire and a perfect side dish is ready.

For serving you can place the couscous in the middle of a platter and add vegetables. From the quails's removed wing tips, necks and offals you can create a sauce so the dish not will not be to dry.

INGREDIENTS PER QUAIL:

1 date

1 shallot

1 slice of bacon

vegetable, according to taste

stock

ras el-hanout seasoning

harissa

QUAILS
WITH DATES AND SHALLOTS

The quails must be prepared for the pot. To do so, cut off the necks and wing tips, which are used later on for the sauce. Salt and pepper the quails and fill each with a date and a shallot. Wrap in a bacon slice and secure with a thread. Sear in the Dutch Oven lid then place on a bed of roasted vegetables inside the Dutch Oven. In the lid, sear the wings and small cut-off parts and add to the pot. Add some stock or water and let cook with the lid closed.

The quail is served with sauce. Remove the quails from the pot and keep them warm on the lid. Then take out all vegetables and bones and boil off the gravy. You can add the strained vegetables back to the pot or thicken the sauce.

A suitable spice is ras el-hanout, a Moroccan seasoning mix. Serve the quails in a bowl on a bed of couscous with the sauce and some harissa.

CASSEROLE RECIPES

ONION TART

Opinions tend to differ when it comes to onion tart. Some like it thickly covered and juicy others like it thinly covered and crispy. This one is thickly covered and juicy and therefore, better suited for baking in the Dutch Oven as the thin tart flambée would require more heat.

INGREDIENTS FOR K8 OR FT6

Pizza dough from 500 g flour (see page 111)

FOR THE TOPPING:

1 kg onions

250 g bacon

caraways

nutmeg

pepper and salt

butter for roasting

1 cup sour cream

2 eggs

Dice the onions and bacon, roast in butter and season with pepper, nutmeg and caraway. Let cool down slightly. Roll out the dough and place in a buttered Loaf Pan k8 or a Dutch Oven ft6. Form an edge of dough of at least two fingers width in height. Pour the roasted onions onto the dough and whisk the eggs with the sour cream. Pour the egg-mixture onto the onions. Grated cheese can be added on top if desired.

Let bake for 30-45 minutes until the dough is done and the mixture has thickened and has turned brown. Use low heat from below and medium heat on top. To gratinate, take the briquettes from below and place them on top of the lid.

QUICHE

INGREDIENTS FOR THE DOUGH

300 g flour

20 g butter

1 egg

1 pinch salt

flour for rolling out

butter for the pan

FOR THE TOPPING

100 g bacon

1 onion

1 leek

4 eggs

250 ml cream

pepper and salt

nutmeg

butter or oil for roasting

For the short pastry pour the flour onto the working surface and form an indentation into which the eggs, salt and cold butter are added. To facilitate kneading the butter it can be cut in small pieces or grated. Knead to a smooth dough, wrap in cling film and let it rest in the refrigerator for half an hour. In the meantime, roast the diced bacon in butter, add the diced onions and sliced leek and roast until translucent.

Roll out the dough on a floured surface and place in an ovenproof pan, also covering its walls. For the topping, mix the eggs and cream and add the roasted mixture of bacon, leek and onions. Generously add pepper and nutmeg. Only salt sparingly, as the bacon is already quite salty itself.

A regular tart case with a diameter of 26 cm will easily fit into an ft6. You should line it with baking paper to facilitate the removal. Let the quiche bake for 30-40 minutes with low bottom heat and medium top heat. The surface should be slightly brown, the filling fully thickened and the base crispy.

Onion tart

BREAD PUDDING WITH WHISKEY SAUCE

A typical pudding, such as the well-known Christmas pudding, consists of flour, fat and dried fruits, somtimes eggs and many excotic spices are added. To shorten baking time people nowadays often use stale white bread, adding an egg-cream-milk mixture as well as various fruits and other ingredients. For a traditional pudding grated beef tallow is used, which has an neutral taste and loosens the batter when distributed evenly. Especially a modern pudding can be easily baked in a normal Dutch Oven.
As the dough will not rise, the mass is well calculable. After baking the pudding is turned out onto a plate. To do so, it is important to thoroughly grease the pan and coat well with breadcrumbs. The mixture is added and should not be moved around anymore inside the pan for not to destroy the coating of butter and breadcrumbs.

INGREDIENTS FOR FT6 OR FT9

½ old white bread or
10 stale small hamburger buns

½ l milk

250 g sugar

1 pinch salt

4 eggs

125 g butter

1 vanilla pod or
1 flask vanilla aroma

1 cinnamon stick

½ tsp. nutmeg

When using a vanilla pod cut it in halves, scrape out the pulp and boil up the pod and pulp in milk for the flavour to develop. The milk must cool down afterwards, otherwise, the eggs will coagulate.
Mix the milk with the spices, sugar, salt and butter and heat up to lukewarm temperature until the butter has molten. Add the eggs and stir well.
Tear the bread into pieces of about 2 x 2 cm. A specific amount is hard to define, as it varies depending on the bread. Place the bread pieces in the milk mixture and briefly knead the dough. The bread pieces should still be identifiable as such and the mass should be humid but not wet.
Put the mixture in a well greased ft6 or ft9 and flatten out the surface.
Let bake at medium top heat and low bottom heat until the pudding is firm but not dry. That should take about 30-45 minutes.

OPTIONS
Add raisins, soaked in rum, to the mixture and use the rum instead of whiskey for the sauce.

WHISKEY SAUCE

DUTCH OVEN OUTDOOR COOKING

INGREDIENTS FOR FT1

250 g sugar

150 g butter

2 cups cream

whiskey to taste
(100-200 ml)

Melt the butter in the Dutch Oven, add the sugar and cream and let everything boil up shortly. To prevent too much alcohol from evaporating add the whiskey a little later.

TORTILLA LASAGNE

Tortillas are one of the most important foods in a kettle drive, which is not only because Tex Mex cooking is widely common but also because the wheat flats are well preservable and versatile in use. The round tortillas are highly suited to be stacked in a Dutch Oven with roasted, minced meat and a spicy sauce, just as you would do for a lasagne. Gratinated with cheese, you easily get a fast and very tasteful meal, prepared in only one pot. The tortillas have softened by soaking up the sauce and its flavour.

INGREDIENTS FOR FT6 OR FT9

8 wheat flour tortillas

2 tins bean purée

1 large jar salsa sauce

FOR THE FILLING

1 kg minced meat (beef or mixed)

2 large onions, finely chopped

2 garlic cloves, finely chopped

chopped jalapeños, as desired

1 large tin tomatoes in pieces

1 large tin kidney beans

1 tin maize

500 g grated cheese, preferably cheddar

fat for roasting

water or stock to deglaze

chilli powder

oregano

pepper and salt

Dissolve some fat in an ft9 and roast the minced meat well crushed apart. Put aside in a separate bowl. Roast the onions, garlic and jalapeños in the ft9 until translucent and soft, then add to the minced meat. Add the tomatoes, beans and maize. In case the mass is too dry, deglaze with some water or stock until it has the consistency of a Chilli con Carne. Finally, add half of the grated cheese and stir well.

For stacking fill some of the mass into the bottom of the Dutch Oven, add a tortillas spread with bean purée, add filling again, followed by a layer of salsa and cheese. Now repeat the layers. The last layer should be filling topped off with abundant cheese. About half to two thirds of the cheese should be sprinkled on top of the lasagne to gratinate. If the cheese was added directly onto a tortilla, without the filling, the dish would become too dry.

For baking heat up the pot with medium bottom heat and wait for the content to boil, then place as many briquettes on the lid as possible to gratinate the cheese.

You can also make your own salsa with a tin of tomatoes, some chilli sauce and finely chopped onions. Top it off by adding some finely chopped jalapenos with some sour liquid from the jar and some sugar.

PASTA BAKE

A pasta bake is always welcome, ideal for using up leftovers and children love it. It should be made more often as it is so easily prepared.

INGREDIENTS FOR K8

300 g pasta

200 g cooked ham

3 eggs

250 ml sour cream

200 g cheese, grated

nutmeg

pepper and salt

Cook the pasta in abundant salted water and let drain. Dice the ham and, in alternation with the pasta, stack it into the Dutch Oven. Whisk the cream with eggs and season with pepper, salt and nutmeg. Finally, top it off with abundant grated cheese, such as Swiss cheese. Let bake with low bottom heat and high top heat until it is heated up properly, the egg-cream mixture thickens, and the cheese is slightly brown.

ROEHRENKLUMP
(POTATO LUMP CASSEROLE)

The wonderful, long-established potato dish has its origins in the area of Brunswick in Southeast-Germany. The name speaks for itself: The potato dough is not baked into pancakes but, as a lump. It is baked in the oven—making it a "Roehrenklump" or "oven lump" and served with sauerkraut. There is also a version in which the sauerkraut is added to the mass and both is baked in a pan in the oven. But then most of the highly desired crust is missing.

Line the Loaf Pan with bacon slices. Grate the potatoes and onions and mix with flour, eggs, pepper and salt. Pour the mass into the pan and cover with some bacon slices.

Let bake for about two hours, with low bottom heat and medium top heat, until the mass has thickened. The bacon fat on top is almost completely dissolved, only some greaves are visible.

INGREDIENTS FOR K4

2 kg potatoes, choose type to taste

4 large onions

4 tbsp. flour

8 eggs

pepper and salt

bacon for the Loaf Pan
(bacon fat if possible)

Shepherd's pie is a typical casserole and extremely tasty when prepared in a Dutch Oven ft3. Working without the lid is possible, but the cheese will not melt as nicely.

INGREDIENTS:

500 g minced meat

500 g potatoes, as mashed potatoes

1 bell pepper

200 g fresh mushrooms

1 onion

200 g cheese, for gratinating

pepper and salt

SHEPHERD'S PIE

Cook the potatoes in abundant salted water, peel and mash to potato purée. Roast the minced meat in some oil. Add and roast the diced onions and bell pepper as well as the sliced mushrooms. Salt and pepper, add some water and cover with mashed potatoes. Sprinkle with cheese, close the lid and gratinate with high top heat until the cheese is brown.

To gratinate, put as many charcoals on the lid as can fit in one layer. However, do remove the pot from the bottom heat, as the ingredients are already cooked.

To melt the cheese in a frying pan it is sufficient to heat up the lid. You can also cover the pan with aluminium foil and put come charcoal on top.

SOUPS & STEWS

INGREDIENTS FOR FT6

600 g potatoes

600 g aubergines

500 g minced meat, lamb if possible

2 onions

2-4 garlic cloves

1 large tin peeled tomatoes, without juice

1 bay leaf

¼ tsp. cinnamon

salt and pepper

4 eggs

3 tbsp. butter

3 tbsp. flour

400 ml milk

100 g parmesan

nutmeg

olive oil for roasting

MOUSSAKA

This aubergine casserole is a little more complex, as many ingredients must be roasted separately, but it's all worth the effort. You can prepare the casserole in advance and bake later, shortly before serving.

Peel the potatoes, cut into 2 mm thick slices and roast in some olive oil, then put aside.
Cut the aubergines into 2 mm thick slices, line a baking tray with paper cloth and spread out the aubergine slices. Salt the aubergine, so they lose water. Roast the slices in olive oil and put aside.

Roast the minced meat in a pan with the finely chopped onions and garlic, add the drained and cut tomatoes and season with cinnamon, bay leaf, nutmeg, pepper and salt. Continuously stirring, let cook until the fluid evaporates, remove the bay leaf and take the pot off the stove. When everything has cooled down a little, stir in two eggs.

Heat up the butter in a pan, cover with flour and let brown slightly. Little by little, add milk, a tablespoon of cheese and season with pepper, salt and nutmeg.

Now the "composition". follows: Grease a Dutch Oven ft6 with olive oil, line the bottom with half of the potato and aubergine slices as well as some cheese. Generously season with pepper, salt and nutmeg and put the minced meat on top. Add a layer of the remaining potato and aubergine slices on top, pour in sauce and add cheese on top.

With low bottom heat and medium top heat the casserole takes about 30-45 minutes to cook.

SAUERKRAUT CASSEROLE

This casserole is a main dish for 4 persons and also a great party dish, that is easily prepared.

INGREDIENTS FOR FT6

1 large tin sauerkraut

250 g ham or bacon dice

500 g minced meat (beef, pork or mixed)

250 ml chilli sauce (alternatively BBQ sauce)

1 onion, diced

2 cups cream

1 cup sour cream

salt, pepper and paprika powder

oil for roasting

250 g grated Edam cheese for gratinating, to your taste

Roast the minced meat in some oil in the Dutch Oven. Add the onion dice. Roast the ham or bacon in the lid, add sauerkraut and chilli sauce and let simmer for some minutes. Pour the mass over the minced meat into the Dutch Oven, add the cream and spices. Let gratinate for about 15-20 minutes, with low heat from below and high top heat. If desired, grated Edam cheese can be used to gratinate.

Yellow, hulled peas soften more quickly.

PEA SOUP

A good pea soup takes time and the right ingredients. Then, however, on a cold, rainy day it is unparalleled in warming up those frozen figures, outdoors by the campfire.

Let the peas soak in water overnight. For yellow peas this is not necessary.

Heat up some fat in the Dutch Oven and roast the diced bacon together with the diced onions. Cut the leek and carrots into rings, dice the celery and pork. Add to the bacon along with the peas in their soaking water and add some more water, if needed. Let cook for at least one or better two hours, add marjoram, pepper and salt and let cook for another 15 minutes.

You can suspend the pot on a Cooking Tripod over the fire or use a Fire Box or the Rocket Stove as energy source. Most importantly the heat must come from below.

INGREDIENTS FOR 8-10 SERVINGS:

750 g peas (dried)

1 kg pork neck or salted and smoked pork

250 g rib bacon

5 onions

2 cups leek

1 cup celery root

1 cup carrots

pepper and salt

marjoram, dried

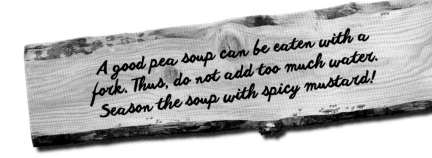

A good pea soup can be eaten with a fork. Thus, do not add too much water. Season the soup with spicy mustard!

CHEESEBURGER SOUP

The soup bears its name as it contains everything that also belongs on a true cheeseburger.

INGREDIENTS FOR 4 SERVINGS:

500 g minced meat, beef or half beef, half pork

1 onion

1 leek

1 l meat stock

250 g mushrooms

120 g soft cheese

1-2 tbsp. flour for thickening

pepper and salt

cayenne pepper, according to taste

Roast the minced meat in some oil until it is dark brown. Add the onion rings and the leek cut in fine half rings. Dust 1-2 tablespoons flour on top and fill up stock. Let simmer for 10 minutes.

In the meantime, roast the sliced mushrooms, add to the soup and let cook for another 5 minutes. Add the cheese and season with salt, pepper and cayenne pepper.

A stew that not only tastes good in winter. For the summer just add a little more liquid, then it will also pass as a vegetable soup. Traditionally, it contains mutton, but if you do not like the taste you can also use lamb shoulder or beef such as prime rib.

IRISH STEW

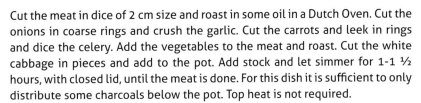

Cut the meat in dice of 2 cm size and roast in some oil in a Dutch Oven. Cut the onions in coarse rings and crush the garlic. Cut the carrots and leek in rings and dice the celery. Add the vegetables to the meat and roast. Cut the white cabbage in pieces and add to the pot. Add stock and let simmer for 1-1 ½ hours, with closed lid, until the meat is done. For this dish it is sufficient to only distribute some charcoals below the pot. Top heat is not required.

Peel and dice the potatoes and let cook in the stew for about 15 minutes. The potatoes will thicken the stew and, depending on the type, make it will remain more fluid or become more creamy. If you find the stew too runny, you can add some sauce thickener. Season with caraways, thyme, nutmeg as well as salt and pepper. Before serving, sprinkle with finely chopped parsley.

INGREDIENTS FOR 4 SERVINGS:

1 kg lamb or beef

2 onions

1 garlic clove

2 carrots

1 cup celery root

2 cups white cabbage

1 cup leek

1 l stock

250 g potatoes

sauce thickener, if needed

1 tsp. caraways

1 tsp. thyme

1 trace nutmeg

pepper and salt

1 tbsp. parsley

FAST LENTIL SOUP

The smart camper plans ahead and in case of emergency has a pot of soup ready to go. Thus, in next to no time a warm, savoury meal will be ready!

Heat up the oil in the pot. Finely dice the onions and roast until translucent. Cut the sausages in slices and roast. When using bacon, roast the bacon before the onions.

As soon as the onions and sausages are roasted, add the lentils and, with the same tin, measure the water to rinse out the remaining lentils. Add sugar and vinegar to taste. Salt is usually not required, but it depends on the meat added. You might need to salt individually.

This dish requires no culinary refinement. The first one placing the pot on the folding table will be the king of the camping kitchen.

INGREDIENTS FOR 1-2 SERVINGS:

(With one person, there will be some leftovers, for two it's possibly not enough, but two tins of lentils are sufficient for three people.)

1 tin lentils (485 ml)

2 ham sausages or some smoked bacon

1 onion

½ tin water

Maggi seasoning, sugar and vinegar, according to taste

oil for roasting

SIDE DISHES

DUTCH OVEN POTATOES

Potatoes from the Dutch Oven are a fast and satisfying side dish. For a less heavy version replace the cream with milk.

You can make the side dish for 15 people when using a Dutch Oven ft12. When adding bacon, you get a delicious main course.

INGREDIENTS PER PERSON

1-2 large potatoes, waxy
½-1 onion
100 g bacon
grated cheese, for gratinating
pepper and salt
1 cup cream

Dice the bacon and onions and slice the peeled potatoes. Put a layer of potatoes into the Dutch Oven, add onions and bacon dice and salt and pepper generously. You can also add other spices, such as hot paprika powder, according to taste. Add another layer of potatoes, followed by bacon and onions and repeat the layers until the final layer of potatoes. Finally, pour in cream to fill half the Dutch Oven.

First, let the potatoes cook in the fluid and steam, by applying medium heat from below. Top heat is not yet required. The potatoes need at least 20 minutes to cook. Only after that time, add the cheese on top and put as many charcoals on top of the lid as possible. Wait for the cheese to melt and turn brown. Serve the Dutch Oven potatoes as hot and fresh as possible. Whether served as side or main course, they are always tasty.

ONION JAM

Onion jam is an ideal addition for hamburgers in the winter. Thanks to the warm jam, the hamburger won't cool down as fast, which is an advantage when it is cold outside.

INGREDIENTS:

onions, red or white
butter
honey or sugar
vinegar
wine, red or white depending on the onions

Depending on the size, cut 3-8 onions in coarse rings, roast in butter and caramelise with honey or sugar. Deglaze with a splash of vinegar and abundant wine—red wine for red onions and white wine for white onions—and let the wine boil down slowly at low heat.

A Dutch Oven ft3 is ideally suited. However, you need to leave the lid open for the wine to evaporate and the mass to thicken.

Sauerkraut is a popular side dish for many wintery recipes. It is a success when prepared in the Dutch Oven but should be removed shortly after cooking to prevent the acid from damaging the patina. It is best to cook a fatty dish afterwards, such as a pork roast with crackling.

SAUERKRAUT

A real sauerkraut requires bacon and onion rings to be roasted first. Only then, the sauerkraut is added. Taste it first and, if very sour, rinse with water to make it milder. Roast the sauerkraut shortly, then add fluid, season to taste and let cook for half an hour with the lid closed. Check if the sauerkraut is done.

When using juniper berries, remember the amount to not forget one when taking them out again. You can also grind them finely, because to bite onto a juniper berry is very unpleasant.

Do not overcook the sauerkraut, tinned sauerkraut is already pre-cooked. For lighter dishes, such as smoked pork or pheasant, a can of pineapple (without juice) conveys a mild flavour to the sauerkraut and wine kraut is accompanied well by grapes. For heavy dishes, such as pork knuckle, the sauerkraut tastes good with bacon or meat juice with fat from the pan.

INGREDIENTS FOR 4 SERVINGS:

500 g sauerkraut

250 g bacon

2 onions

wine (for wine sauerkraut)
or stock/gravy

juniper berries, according to taste

if desired, pineapple or grapes

A perfect ingredient for sauerkraut is stock or gravy. If you have none leftover from another dish you can use some ready-made.

Polenta

POLENTA

In every culture there is a main dish made of corn and polenta is one of them. You need a high Dutch Oven (ft9) and a strong, long spoon to be able to stir vigorously. Polenta made only of maize semolina is not very appealing which is why you should add stock to the water.

INGREDIENTS:

600 g maize semolina

1 ½ l warm water

2 l stock

2 tbsp. salt

200 g parmesan

Pour the water into a high Dutch Oven. Add the salt and maize semolina and boil up by stirring continuously. The polenta will thicken. Little by little, fill in stock until the creamy consistency of the typical Italian polenta is achieved. This will take about 40 minutes, but the continuous stirring will pay off.

Traditionally, polenta is poured directly into middle of the table on the wooden plate and topped with meat or mushroom tomato sauce and sprinkled with parmesan.

MEALIE-PAP
(MAIZE MASH)

A simple side dish and staple food for almost the entire African continent. The dish is known under many different names, depending on the respective region in Africa. Also the recipes might differ slightly.

INGREDIENTS:

1 ½ l water

500 g maize flour (fine as powder, white)

salt

1 stock cube

butter

Put the crumbled stock cube and some salt into a pot with cold water. Then pour the flour into the cold water and whisk vigorously until there are no more lumps visible.

Place the pot on the fire and boil up the stock while whisking continuously. After some time, when the flour swells and the mash thickens, replace the whisk with a wooden spoon. If the dish becomes too thick, add some water and if it is too runny, add flour. If desired, add some butter shortly before serving.

A general rule for the mixing ratio: One cup of flour for two cups of water always works!

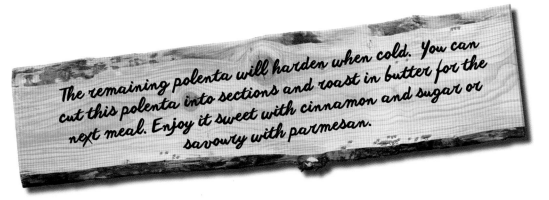

The remaining polenta will harden when cold. You can cut this polenta into sections and roast in butter for the next meal. Enjoy it sweet with cinnamon and sugar or savoury with parmesan.

Bayrisch Kraut

INGREDIENTS FOR 6 SERVINGS:

1 kg white cabbage

200 g rib bacon

1 onion

2 tbsp. lard for roasting

½ l stock

1 splash vinegar

pepper and salt

1 tbsp. sugar

caraways, to taste, but at least
1 tbsp.

BAYRISCH KRAUT
(BAVARIAN CABBAGE)

 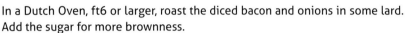

In a Dutch Oven, ft6 or larger, roast the diced bacon and onions in some lard. Add the sugar for more brownness.
Cut the cabbage into thin slices and also add to the pot. Roast until it collapses. Add the stock and season well with vinegar, pepper, salt and caraways. After 30-40 minutes, the Bavarian cabbage should be soft and, yet, still firm.

Due to the acid, the dish must quickly be removed from the cast-iron pot and transferred into another container. It should never be left in the pot overnight.

RED CABBAGE

Freshly prepared red cabbage is a delicacy! Still, only few people take the trouble, even though it is great when cooked to the point.

Cut the fresh red cabbage in very thin stripes. Heat up the onions in some oil in the Dutch Oven. Roast the red cabbage in portions until it collapses. Pour the red cabbage and finely diced apples into the pot and add some stock or water and vinegar. Pepper and salt as well as a pinch of sugar are a must. Other possible spices are cloves and pimento as well as the mandatory bay leaf, just as you prefer.

INGREDIENTS:

1 red cabbage

onions

1 apple (Boskoop)

stock or water

3 tbsp. vinegar

pepper and salt

1 pinch sugar

cloves

pimento

1 bay leaf

BAKED POTATOES

The best baked potatoes are prepared in a Dutch Oven. The trick is to place the large potatoes onto a bed of salt. Thus, the heat is distributed more evenly, and the potatoes are not burned at the contact surface below. If you like to add some more flavour, melt butter with some salt in a pan and roast some whole, slightly crushed garlic cloves. Draw up this aromatic butter in a marinade injector and inject into the already soft potatoes. Let the injected potatoes rest for ten more minutes.

No salt at hand? Fine sand is also suitable, but the potatoes must then be cleaned thoroughly before serving! Sugar cannot be used, as it melts and caramelises. You can also place the potatoes on a cast or stack grate.

POTATO GRATIN

A good potato gratin is an always welcome side dish.

INGREDIENTS PER PERSON:

1 large potato

½ onion

approx. 100 ml cream

approx. 50 g Swiss cheese

pepper and salt

nutmeg

Cut the potatoes and onions into slices and mix in a medium sized Dutch Oven. Add salt and pepper, some nutmeg and the cream. First cook the potatoes with bottom heat until soft. Put as many charcoals below the Dutch Oven that the sauce simmers. Grate the cheese over the gratin and let gratinate at high top heat. Put as many charcoals on the lid as can fit in one layer.

SWEET FRIED POTATOES

Sweet fried potatoes are a delicacy as side or main dish. On the eve of the meal cook plenty of plum-sized, waxy potatoes and let cool. On the next day peel the potatoes when they are nicely greasy.

In a Fire Skillet that holds all potatoes side by side, roast the potatoes in some lard or clarified butter. As soon as the potatoes are brown and hot all around, sprinkle abundant sugar on top. Now, stir quickly and intensely to ensure that the sugar caramelises everywhere and at the same time loses it sweetness.

Sweet fried potatoes

INGREDIENTS:

4 stale rolls (from the previous day, soft and sticky, not hard!)

1 cup flour

3 eggs

milk or water

pepper and salt

1 pinch nutmeg

parsley, to taste

BREAD DUMPLINGS

Bread dumplings are a perfect way to use up leftovers and are a tasty side dish for goulash or roulades.

Tear the soft rolls in approximately cherry-sized pieces. In a large bowl, mix the rolls with flour, eggs and spices. Little by little, add milk or water to create a loose mass that sticks well together. This best done by means of a dough scraper. With damp hands, form dumplings in the size of golf or tennis balls. These can be prepared several hours before the meal and, then, cooked freshly.

Cook the dumplings in a Dutch Oven with salted water until they rise up to the surface.

When adding roasted bacon dice, you get bacon dumplings. These used to be a main dish rather then a side dish.

GRATINATED CHEESE

The small Dutch Oven ft3 is perfectly suited to prepare appetisers, such as gratinated cheese.

For the feta version, take a 400 g piece feta, some olives, chilli, garlic to taste, onion rings and gyro seasoning. Put everything onto the cheese and pour a generous amount of olive oil on top. Let bake at low heat from below and high top heat until the first onion tips turn black and the cheese has completely lost its shape. Place the pot on the table and everyone self serves some on their white bread.

For the Camembert version, put a fatty, round Camembert into the pot and let it melt slowly at high top heat. As soon as the surface turns brown, cut the skin crosswise and fold back the corners, to brown the inside.
You can, in addition, also bake the cheese wrapped in puff pastry. Serve with cranberries and toast.

To gratinate, put as many charcoals on the lid as can be fit in one layer.

Camembert

Feta

Chanterelles

CHANTERELLES

Plentiful mushrooms at the open fire are a special delicacy, especially when they are self-gathered. For chanterelles, it is important to roast them in high temperature fat, as they develop their typical flavour at temperatures well above 100 °C.

INGREDIENTS PER SERVING:

200-300 g chanterelles

1 small onion

50 g smoked bacon

pepper and salt

cream, if desired

clarified butter, for roasting

Put some clarified butter into the pan and roast the diced bacon. Add the chanterelles and let roast. Add the onions and roast until translucent, then add salt and pepper. While stirring continuously, let the mushrooms simmer in fat until the simmering stops.

MUSHROOM PAN

While grilling, a mushroom pan as a vegetarian snack or side dish is a delight.

INGREDIENTS PER SERVING:

200-300 g fresh mushrooms, not too large

1 onion

100 g herb butter

Heat up a large Fire Skillet and put in the herb butter. Add the mushrooms and onion dice and that's it! As soon as simmering stops and the mushrooms get colour, the mushroom pan is ready. They are a delight served with fresh baguette.

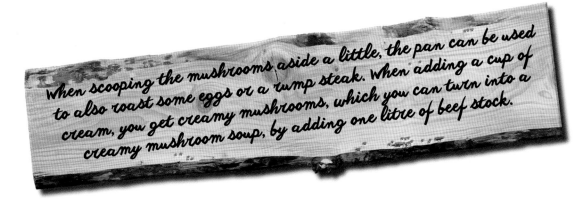

When scooping the mushrooms aside a little, the pan can be used to also roast some eggs or a rump steak. When adding a cup of cream, you get creamy mushrooms, which you can turn into a creamy mushroom soup, by adding one litre of beef stock.

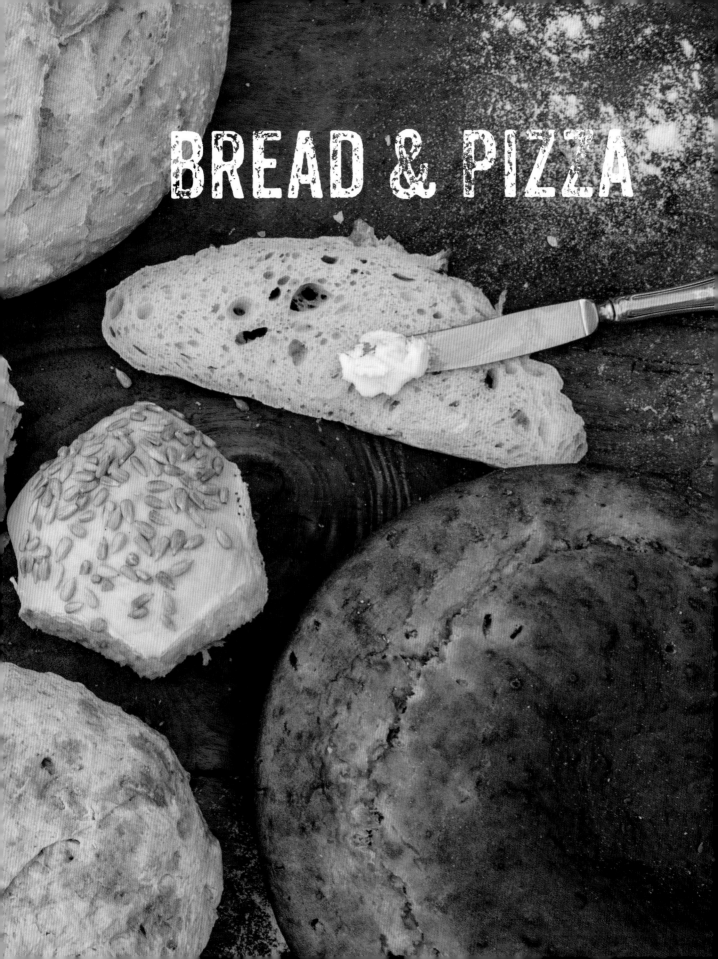

BREAD & PIZZA

MAIZE BREAD

INGREDIENTS FOR FT6 OR FT9

2 cups maize flour (no polenta, but finely ground white flour!)

2 cups grated cheddar

2 cups soft flour

2 tbsp. sugar

1 tsp. salt

1 pack baking powder

4 slightly whisked eggs

4 tbsp. oil

3 cups milk

If desired, diced jalapenos

Mix the maize flour, soft flour, cheese and other dry ingredients in a bowl. In a second bowl, whisk the eggs with oil and milk. Mix the dry and wet ingredients until you have a smooth batter (similar to pancake batter). You can add chopped chilli to the batter if you like.

For baking, it is important to previously heat up the Dutch Oven as high as possible, thus, to ensure that the dough immediately develops a crust and won't stick on. Therefore, initially, put all charcoals below the Dutch Oven. Then let bake in a Dutch Oven ft6 or ft9 at high top heat and medium bottom heat. Make sure to reduce the bottom heat after heating up and pouring in the batter. After 30 minutes, check if the bread has set.

RYE BREAD

INGREDIENTS:

600 g rye flour

300 g plain flour

2 pack dry yeast

2 packs sourdough

3 tsp. salt

Mix all ingredients and gradually add water. Knead the dough until it has the right consistency—a little more than humid but also not as runny as for pancakes. Cover the bowl and let the dough rise at a warm place to double in size.

Take out the dough and briefly knead into form, for not to squeeze out too much air, and put it into the Loaf Pan. Let rise in the pan a second time, then let bake for 30-45 minutes. Use a thermometer to check if it is done. The bread is done at a temperature of 98 °C and when no more dough sticks to the thermometer when pulled out. You can also use a wood stick to check. Remove the bread from the Pan and let cool down on a grate.

You can also check the bread by tapping the bottom side. If it sounds hollow the bread is done.

Rye bread

INGREDIENTS FOR FT6 OR FT9

500 g very strong flour or, even bet-ter, freshly ground, coarse whole-meal

2 tsp. baking soda

3 tbsp. butter

350 ml buttermilk

1 tsp. sugar

IRISH SODA BREAD

Ireland has a tradition of baking bread with soda (baking soda). The Irish used to be very poor, especially in rural areas and such a bread was a nice alternative to the dull cereal porridge. The quality of the flour is of high importance, as it is decisive for the taste of the bread, which contains only few other ingredients.

Preheat the Dutch Oven with low bottom heat and medium top heat. Put all dry ingredients and the butter into a bowl and knead in the butter until it is no longer visible. Add buttermilk until you have a smooth dough, which is not runny anymore. As the flour quality is decisive on how much fluid the dough takes up, the beforementioned amount is only a guideline and, you may use more or less, just as needed.

Form a round loaf and place it inside the greased and floured Dutch Oven. Deeply cut the surface crosswise. Spray water on the surface and the insides of the Dutch Oven to generate a humid climate. After 40-45 minutes, the loaf should be well done and produce a hollow sound when tapped. Tear the bread into four parts, along the crosswise cut and serve warm with butter and jam, for instance together with a hot tea.

FOLDED BREAD

A folded bread is a typical party dish as the folds are easy to divide and portion.

There are no limits when topping the bread. A simple herb butter is a good start and roasted bacon and onion dice are an option.

INGREDIENTS FOR LOAF PAN K4

600 g flour (pizza flour or plain flour, soft flour if no other available)
300 ml lukewarm water
2 tsp. salt
1 tsp. sugar
500 ml olive oil
1 pack dry yeast
For coating: 250 g herb butter

Mix the dry ingredients for the dough, add the oil and knead well to evenly distribute the oil. Add the water and knead the dough until it strips off the bowl and has a smooth and elastic consistency. Cover and let rise until it has doubled in size.

Afterwards, knead very briefly and roll out into a rectangle to cut into stripes, which have the width of the Loaf Pan's inside. Coat the dough stripes with herb butter and, in folds, put into the greased pan, fill it up to about ⅔. In the pan, the dough should rise a second time, before baking it with eight briquettes on top and four below. Depending on the weather and outside temperature, the bread should be done after 45-60 minutes.

The folded bread tastes best when still warm directly from pan.

HAMBURGER BUNS FROM THE DUTCH OVEN

Soft buns are a must for pulled pork or hamburgers. Depending on the size of the Dutch Oven the buns should be baked in several steps. These buns are perfect to be grilled on the cut surface and, thus, will not soak as fast with a very juicy patty on top.

INGREDIENTS FOR 10-12 PIECES

500 g plain flour

200 ml water

50 ml milk

1 egg

100 g butter

1 tbsp. sugar

1 tsp. salt

1 pack dry yeast or ½ dice fresh yeast

FOR COATING AND SPRINKLING

1 egg

sesame

Put the dry ingredients into a bowl. Heat up the milk, water and finely cut butter until the butter melts. By heating up the milk water mixture the dough will get its required temperature. Add the liquid and egg to the dry ingredients and knead a smooth dough that strips off the bowl. If necessary, adjust the dough's consistency with some milk or flour. Let the dough rise at a warm place for about an hour, until doubled in size. Afterwards, knead the dough very briefly and form 10-12 balls of the same size. Roll these balls on the table to add some tension to the dough. Now, put the buns at some distance into the greased Dutch Oven, press flat and let rise a second time. Before baking, coat the surface with whisked egg and sprinkle sesame on top.

After 15-20 minutes at medium top and bottom heat the buns should be done and can cool down on a grate.

STICK BREAD

For children, stick bread is the best part of a campfire. Here are some tips how to make it quick and easy.

INGREDIENTS FOR 12-15 PIECES

Pizza dough, basic recipe on page 111

Wrap the dough in long spirals around the end of the stick. The dough should not be thicker than a small finger, as it does not fully bake, otherwise. When using the Petromax Campfire Skewers wrap the dough in several eighth around the end, as shown in the picture.

For baking, it is important to hold the dough over a bed of glowing embers or lateral to the radiating heat of the fire and not directly over the flames. It is best to lay the skewers on a support holding them above the bed of glowing embers and only turn them once. As soon as the dough has risen and turned golden brown you can enjoy the bread with some butter and salt.

Stick bread

BANNOCK

Bannock is the bread of the wild. It is always prepared at the open fire.

INGREDIENTS PER SERVING:

2 cups flour

1 tsp. baking powder

½ tsp. salt

1 tbsp. fat or oil

With flour, some water, salt, fat and baking powder, prepare a firm dough that strips off the bowl. Knead well for three minutes and form a round, flat loaf, approx. 0.5 cm thick. Heat up some fat in the pan and bake the bannock from both sides, until golden brown. Bannock tastes best when fresh and warm.

But even better than a bannock is a sour dough bannock. Take one cup of flour less than for regular ones and add a cup of sourdough, instead. When making bannocks more often, get a sourdough starter at the bakery and mix with a cup of water and two tablespoons of flour. After two days at a warm place, the sourdough is bubbly and ready to use. Replace the amount you take with water and flour.

Please remember: Bannock is never cut but only broken apart, as it would bring bad luck otherwise!

Bannock can be prepared in any type of pan, whether it is cast-iron or wrought-iron, or on the Fire Bowl.

BASIC PIZZA DOUGH

PIZZA ROLLS

INGREDIENTS FOR ABOUT 4-6 PIZZA BASES (DEPENDING ON SIZE AND THICKNESS)

500 g plain flour

1 pack dry yeast

1 ½ tbsp. sugar

300 ml lukewarm water

3 tbsp. olive oil

2 tsp. salt

Sift the flour into a bowl, mix with the oil and dry ingredients and add the lukewarm water. Knead the dough until it strips off the bowl, cover it and let rest at a warm place for one hour until the dough has doubled in size. Another possibility is cold fermentation, letting the dough rise in the refrigerator or at room temperature for 4-6 hours. Thus, it is much easier to handle than when applying the fast method at a warm place.

Knead the risen dough again, as wheat dough (in contrast to rye dough) improves with every kneading. Form apple-sized balls, roll out and lift the edges slightly to prevent the topping from running down. Choose the topping according to taste.

First, spread a thin(!) layer of tomato sauce onto the dough. Add thin slices of mozzarella and fresh basil leaves to the pizza. When having a pizza with different toppings, put everything on top except for the fresh mushrooms or salami (are to be put on top of the cheese), then add oregano followed by cheese, mushrooms and the salami.

Rolls from the day before can be made into delicious pizza rolls. There are no limits for topping ideas.

INGREDIENTS FOR FT6 OR FT9

6-8 rolls

500 g soured cream

250 g Swiss cheese, grated

250 g salami

250 g cooked ham

1-2 bell pepper

oregano or pizza seasoning

pepper and salt

In a bowl, mix the soured cream with cheese, finely diced bell pepper, salami and cooked ham. Season with oregano or pizza seasoning and pepper. Taste before adding salt, as salami and ham already contain quite an amount of salt. Cut the rolls in halves and generously spread the mixture on top. Place the halves inside the Dutch Oven (works in several portions) and bake at low bottom heat and high top heat until softened and brown.

CAKES, PASTRY & DESSERT

KIRSCHMICHEL
(CHERRY BREAD PUDDING)

For this dish any left-over rolls or white bread are used up.

INGREDIENTS FOR DUTCH OVEN FT6

400 ml milk, possibly more

5 rolls from the previous day or the same amount of white bread

2 jars cherries, drained, fresh or frozen cherries are also suitable

3 eggs

2 tbsp. sugar

2 tbsp. vanilla sugar

1 lemon, grated peel

2 tbsp. butter

½ tsp. cinnamon

salt

butter flakes and almond flakes, for topping

Cut the rolls in slices as thick as a finger and pour over some lukewarm milk. Turn the rolls from time to time to make sure they soak with milk evenly.
Separate the eggs and whisk up the egg white with a pinch of salt. In another bowl, melt the butter and whisk together with sugar, vanilla sugar, egg yolk and lemon peel until frothy. Add the cherries and rolls and mix carefully. Fold in the egg white and pour everything into a greased Dutch Oven ft6. Sprinkle cinnamon and almond flakes on top and add abundant butter flakes.
Let bake for about 45 minutes with low bottom heat and medium top heat. It tastes best warm from the pot with vanilla sauce.

PANCAKES

Pancakes are always welcome, not only for children! Whether for breakfast or as dessert, everyone loves pancakes. They can be prepared sweet or savoury. The batter is quickly prepared, using a whisk or even a fork.

INGREDIENTS FOR ABOUT 8 PIECES:

2 cups milk (½ l)

2 cups flour

4 eggs

1 tbsp. oil

2 tbsp. sugar

1 tsp. salt

fat, for roasting

AS GARNISH:

bacon, if desired

jam

chocolate spread

cinnamon and sugar

Slowly, add the flour and the other ingredients to the milk until you have a smooth, somewhat viscous pancake batter. For baking, put some butter or oil into the pan and a portion of the dough. Do not turn the pancakes until they come off the bottom. It is easiest if you place a lid or plate on top and flip it. Afterwards, let the pancake slide from the plate back into the pan.

Bacon buckwheat pancakes

BACON BUCKWHEAT PANCAKES

SKILLETS · OUTDOOR COOKING

These pancakes used to be the typical breakfast in poorer regions of Lower Saxony in Germany and were called "Bookwieten-Janhinnerk." Traditionally, they contained three stripes of bacon, even four for dear guests. Instead of milk they are prepared with black coffee. They are served with sugy beet molasses or jam.

INGREDIENTS FOR 16 PIECES

1 kg buckwheat flour

2 l liquid (1 l cold coffee, 1 l water)

8 eggs

salt

48 slices bacon, 3 for each pancake

oil or lard for roasting

sugar beet juice, to serve

Prepare a batter with the flour and the other ingredients, adding the entire coffee and the water only slowly, to adjust the consistency of the batter. Let the batter rest for 2 hours for the flour to soak.

Put three bacon slices into the pan and roast from both sides, then place in the middle of the pan in an even distance. If necessary, add more fat or oil to the pan and add a ladle full of batter to the pan to completely cover the bottom and the bacon slices. For turning, place a plate on top of the pancake inside the pan, flip the pan over and let the pancakes slide back into the pan.

BLUEBERRY PANCAKES

The pancakes have about the size of beer coasters to leave room on the plate for other treats. The fresh blueberries are baked into the batter, but only sparingly to ensure the bound consistency. If you only have tinned blueberries, pour them on top of the pancakes after baking.

INGREDIENTS FOR ABOUT 8 PIECES:

2 cups flour

400 ml butter milk

2 eggs

1-2 tbsp. sugar, to taste

1 tbsp. baking powder

fresh bilberries/blueberries

maple syrup

butter for roasting

Prepare a pancake batter with flour, butter milk, eggs, sugar and baking powder. Add cleaned blueberries to the batter. Heat up some butter in a pan and use a ladle to fill in some batter, to form pancakes of beer coaster size. Make sure to add some blueberries to every portion.

KAISERSCHMARRN

Kaiserschmarrn is a classic Austrian recipe. In Austrian cooking pastries play an important role. The dish is served with lots of icing sugar.

Separate the eggs and whisk up the egg white with half the sugar. In a second bowl, whisk the flour with egg yolk, milk, the second half of sugar and salt until frothy. Add the beaten egg white to the batter and fold in.

Let the butter foam in the pan and add the entire pancake batter. Sprinkle the raisins on top. As soon as the batter browns at the bottom, flip over the Kaiserschmarrn. When the other side browns, tear apart the Kaiserschmarrn into bite-sized pieces, using two forks, and sprinkle with icing sugar. Serve with apple sauce.

INGREDIENTS:

1 ½ cups flour (200 g)

1 ¼ cups milk (300 ml)

100 g sugar

4 eggs

2 tbsp. raisins

1 pinch salt

icing sugar, to sprinkle

2 tbsp. butter, for roasting

apple sauce

RICE PUDDING IN A THERMOS

Rice pudding is a simple dish, made from one part rice (risotto rice or special round-grain rice for rice pudding) and two parts milk. This recipe is very suitable for travellers, as the ingredients have a low weight and will not spoil, especially when using milk powder to prepare milk on the spot. In the USA rice pudding is cooked with some raisins and called "spotted dog," resembling the spots on the fur of a Dalmatian.

INGREDIENTS PER SERVING AS MAIN DISH:

1 cup rice

2 cups milk

sugar, according to taste

some raisins

sugar and cinnamon, to sprinkle

melted butter, according to taste

fresh fruits

maple syrup

Slowly boil up the rice in milk with sugar in a small Dutch Oven then let simmer for 10 minutes. Fill the mass into a pre-heated thermos with wide neck. After some hours, the rice has soaked some more and can be eaten with sugar and cinnamon, melted butter or maple syrup, either as main dish or dessert. The thermos easily holds the rice pudding, to be eaten still warm on a hike or at the place of destination.

BAKED APPLES

Apples are available basically everywhere and perfect to make baked apples, a sadly forgotten dessert. Depending on your equipment they can be prepared in a Dutch Oven or even in a tin placed next to the campfire.

Remove the apple core and fill the hole to your taste with nuts, marzipan, jam or cranberries. Finally, coat with sugar or honey and cook until the apple collapses slightly. Enjoy hot, with vanilla sauce, liquid cream or sweet condensed milk.

Baked apples from the Dutch Oven prepared at the campfire are a delicious and inexpensive dish, not only when having children around.

Baked apples

CHEESECAKE

A juicy cheesecake is an always welcome dessert. By using butter biscuits as base the recipe is easy to follow, even if you are rather at odds with cake baking so far.

INGREDIENTS FOR FT6, FT9 OR FT12

FOR THE CAKE BASE:

250 g butter biscuits

75 g butter

2 tbsp. sugar

FOR THE TOPPING:

500 g plain curd

300 g plain yoghurt

50 g butter

1 pack vanilla sugar

1 lemon (untreated)

6 eggs

150 g sugar

1 pinch salt

icing sugar

For the base cover the inside of a Dutch Oven with baking paper. The paper should protrude at the sides to facilitate later lifting out of the cake. Put the biscuits into a plastic bag and crush them into fine crumbs by means of a cast-iron Fire Skillet. Pour the crumbs into a bowl, add sugar and melted butter. Distribute the mass as cake base in the Dutch Oven.

For the topping, mix the melted butter, vanilla sugar, lemon juice, grated lemon peel and the sugar in a bowl. Separate the eggs and pour the yolks into the mixture. In a separate bowl, whisk the egg whites with a pinch of salt.

Stir in the yoghurt and curd, add the beaten egg whites and fold in until a smooth mass develops. Pour it onto the cake base inside the Dutch Oven and spread with a scraper.

For baking, you need low bottom heat and strong top heat. Check after 30 minutes how far the cake is done and adjust the heat, if needed. Do not forget to turn the lid by a quarter every 10 minutes to have an evenly brown surface. The cake should be done after 40-45 minutes. Let the cake cool down inside the Dutch Oven to prevent it from collapsing when lifted out.

MUG CAKE

These mug cakes are a recipe for the modern minimalist kitchen, that manages only with a microwave. They are also perfect to be prepared in the Petromax Mugs inside the Dutch Ovens.

INGREDIENTS FOR 6 MUGS IN FT6 OR FT9

200 g soft flour

200 g butter

300 g sugar

400 ml milk

6 eggs

6 tbsp. cacao powder

2 tsp. baking powder

Melt the butter in a bowl, stir in the other ingredients and whisk to a homogeneous mass. Distribute the batter into six mugs.

In a Dutch Oven the cakes are baked at medium heat from below and above for about 10 minutes. You can press a piece of couverture or dark chocolate into the batter in the mugs, before baking to obtain a fluid chocolate core. Use a stick to test if the cakes are done. Of course, the stick test does not work when having baked in a piece of chocolate in the centre for a fluid core.

Mug cake

NUT CAKE

A juicy nut cake is always a pleasure and stays fresh for several days. It can be prepared in the Loaf Pan k4 as well as in a Dutch Oven ft4.5, ft6 or ft9.

INGREDIENTS FOR FT6 OR FT9

FOR THE BATTER:

250 g soft flour

250 g butter

250 g ground hazelnuts

200 g sugar

4 eggs

1 pack vanilla sugar

1 pack baking powder

1 pinch salt

125 ml milk

FOR THE ICING:

chocolate coating

hazelnuts, coarsely chopped

Whisk the warm butter with sugar and vanilla sugar, then stir in the eggs, one by one. Mix the flour with the salt and baking powder and fold it into the butter-sugar mass until the flour is no longer visible. Finally, add the hazelnuts and milk in portions until you have a smooth batter. Observe the consistency of the batter, which should not be too runny. Bake with low bottom heat and medium top heat for about 60 minutes until the stick test shows that the cake is done.

Let the cake cool down inside the pan, lift it out and coat with melted chocolate. As garnish sprinkle with coarsely chopped hazelnuts so they stick to the still liquid chocolate.

BANANA BREAD

Banana bread is no bread in the proper sense but rather a solid cake eaten with butter and honey. It requires a relatively long baking time and, thus, is better baked in a Loaf Pan without lid, within a Dutch Oven ft12.

INGREDIENTS FOR K4 IN FT12

250 g soft flour

150 g sugar

75 g oat flakes

50 ml sunflower oil

100 ml milk

2 eggs

3 very ripe bananas

1 pack baking powder

2 tsp. cinnamon

1 tsp. salt

vanilla aroma or vanilla pulp

First, preheat the ft12 at medium heat from below and above. A cast-iron grate on the inside is helpful. Cover the inside of the Loaf Pan with baking paper.

In a bowl, mix all dry ingredients (flour, sugar, oat flakes, baking powder, cinnamon and salt) well. In another bowl, pulp the bananas with a fork and add the other wet ingredients (oil, milk, eggs). As soon as everything is well mixed, add the dry ingredients little by little and roughly stir with a wooden spoon. When no more flour is visible, fill the batter into the Loaf Pan and immediately place it into the preheated ft12. The baking time is about one hour. However, check after about 45 minutes if the cake is done by means of the stick test. The banana bread should be juicy, which is easy to achieve when covering the pan with aluminium foil while the cake is cooling down, to keep the moisture from escaping.

SCONES

Scones are a traditional British pastry which is freshly baked preferably at the open peat fire and eaten with jam and cream at teatime.

INGREDIENTS FOR FT6 OR FT9

2 ½ cups soft flour

1 cup ginger ale

1 pack baking powder

2 tbsp. cream

1 egg

2 tbsp. brown sugar

1 pinch salt

SERVE WITH:

freshly whipped, cold cream

jam

clotted cream (alternatively crème double)

The trick with scones is to knead them only briefly which makes their preparation perfectly suitable for the campfire.
First, mix the flour and baking powder in a bowl. Make an indentation into the flour where the remaining ingredients are poured. Quickly mix the ingredients and partition off pieces of golf ball size. With your hands form them to balls and shortly roll them in flour. Put a Cast-Iron Trivet or Stack Grate with aluminium foil or baking paper on top into the preheated ft6 or ft9.
Place the scones inside the Dutch Oven and coat them with some milk or yolk. The scones should be done after 15 minutes with medium bottom heat and strong top heat. Use a stick or fork to test if they are done. Scones do not appeal much to the eye, with their uneven form and spiky surface, but that is quite normal. Let the scones cool down shortly and enjoy them still warm with a cup of tea. The scones are served cut in halves with butter or cream and jam spread on top.

RING CAKE

Originally, the ring cake is a poor man's cake that is traditionally prepared with yeast to save eggs. This recipe, however, contains baking powder and lots of eggs.

INGREDIENTS

500 g soft flour

350 g sugar

250 g soft butter

100 ml milk

1 pack vanilla sugar

5 eggs

1 pack baking powder

2 tbsp. raisins, as desired

butter for the pan

First, grease the Ring Cake Pan with abundant butter. Whisk the soft butter with the sugar and vanilla sugar until frothy. Add the eggs, one by one. Mix the flour and baking powder and add it in portions and in alternation with the milk. Finally, fold in raisins, if desired. When the batter is smooth pour it into the pan.

Bake the Ring Cake in an ft12 or ft18 with low bottom heat and medium top heat without the lid on the Ring Cake Pan as the batter will still rise well. It is possible to heat the Ring Cake Pan directly with briquettes but, you should then divide the batter and bake in two portions.

TART CASE

A delicious tart case covered with fresh fruits is always a delight, especially in the summer.

INGREDIENTS

4 tbsp. soft flour

4 tbsp. sugar

4 tbsp. oil

2 eggs

1 tsp. baking powder

1 pinch salt

breadcrumbs and butter for the pan

Preheat a Dutch Oven ft6 or ft9. Grease the lid of the Ring Cake Pan with butter and cover with breadcrumbs.
In a bowl mix all ingredients to a smooth batter. Pour the batter into the Tart Case Lid and place the pan inside the Dutch Oven. The Dutch Oven is heated with medium top and bottom heat. The cake should be done after 10-15 minutes. Let it cool down and add topping to your taste.

CINNAMON ROLLS

Any restaurant has a house speciality and if there really is a speciality among Dutch Oven bakers then it clearly is cinnamon rolls. Not only does this dish taste good, but it also requires a certain skill and looks just fantastic. Therefore to some extent, perfect cinnamon rolls stand for a knightly accolade for campfire baking.

Let the yeast and sugar dissolve in a cup of warm milk. Pour the flour into a bowl. Make an indentation in the flour and add the dissolved yeast. Knead in the yeast, starting at the edges and add the remaining milk until you have a smooth dough. Let the dough rise for 10 minutes. Add the remaining ingredients and knead well until you have a firm and smooth dough that strips off the bowl. Let it rise for one hour until it has doubled in size.

Mix the ingredients for the filling and place a baking paper in the Dutch Oven, protruding at the sides, which will facilitate taking the cinnamon rolls out later.

Flatly roll out the dough and spread the filling on top. Roll up the dough and cut the roll into thick slices, which are aligned upright in the Dutch Oven. Let the dough rise once more until it has doubled again. Before baking, coat the cinnamon rolls with egg yolk. Bake the cinnamon rolls for 30-40 minutes until they are golden, with low bottom heat and strong top heat.

You can enjoy the warm cinnamon rolls directly out of the Dutch Oven with vanilla sauce or you let them cool down, take them out and spread apricot jam on top to make them look shiny. You can glaze them with a mixture of orange juice and icing sugar.

Ingredients for the dough	ft4.5	ft6 / ft9	ft12	ft18
flour	333 g	500 g	750 g	1000 g
milk	170 ml	250 ml	375 ml	500 ml
sugar	50 g	75 g	110 g	150 g
melted butter	50 g	75 g	110 g	150 g
yeast	1 ½ pack	1 pack	1 ½ pack	2 packs
salt	1 pinch	1 pinch	1 pinch	1 pinch

For the filling	ft4.5	ft6 / ft9	ft12	ft18
butter	40 g	60 g	90 g	120 g
brown sugar	50 g	75 g	110 g	150 g
coconut flakes	50 g	75 g	110 g	150 g
raisins	50 g	75 g	110 g	150 g
rum	as desired	as desired	as desired	as desired
cinnamon	½ tsp.	1 tsp.	1 ½ tsp.	2 tsp.
cacao powder	1 tbsp.	1 tbsp.	1 ½ tbsp.	2 tbsp.

Be creative when preparing the filling. If you don't like co- conut flakes you can also use chopped almonds, roasted oat flakes or chocolate spread with cherries or cherry jam. Let the raisins soak in rum, overnight. You can also prepare a savoury dough without sugar and fill the rolls with bacon, onions and cheese.

DRINKS

CHAI

Chai is a spicy tea with milk that originates from India and has made its way to Europe and the US as the beverage of scouts, sometimes substituting the milk with a heavy red wine. The preparation is usually accompanied by various rituals to expel evil spirits.

ORIGINAL RECIPE:

1 l water

½ l milk

3 tbsp. Darjeeling tea

3 tbsp. sugar

1 tbsp. ginger powder

1 tbsp. cardamom pods

Boil the milk together with water and add the spices and tea. Let simmer for five minutes and strain into the cups. Add sugar according to taste.

SCOUTS' RECIPE:

2 l black tea, tea leaves removed

1 l red wine

honey, according to taste

1 cup raisins

1 cinnamon stick

1 tsp. cloves

Add the red wine and the other ingredients to the hot tea and heat up to about 80°C. Garnish with raisins, according to taste.

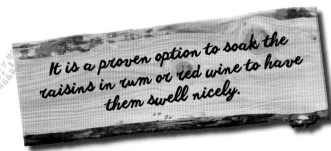

It is a proven option to soak the raisins in rum or red wine to have them swell nicely.

INGREDIENTS PER CUP:

hot water

rum according to taste

sugar

GROG

"Rum is a must, sugar a might and water not needed"—that is the best way to describe a grog. In the past, half a litre of rum was part of the daily ration on board of a sailing vessel. To prevent the sailors from drinking all the rum at once it was mixed with three times the amount of boiled water. Sometimes, a lemon slice was added to prevent scurvy, a deficiency desease of the time.

Heat up the water, add rum and sugar and your grog is ready!
A grog with whiskey and a pea-sized piece of butter on top is known as a toddy and definitely worth a try.

SPICY MULLED WINE

per litre of wine or juice:

1 star anise

5 cloves

1 cinnamon stick

1 tsp. ground, dried ginger

sugar, according to taste and depending on the sweetness of the wine or juice

MULLED WINE

Many cultures know hot, alcoholic beverages: In Nordic countries, the Vikings' descendants heated up Met, in Frankfurt one has hot apple wine and for kids hot apple juice is a great beverage.

Add the spices to the Dutch Oven and slowly heat up the wine to approximately 80 °C.

FRUIT MULLED WINE

Per litre of wine:

1 orange, sliced

1 lemon, sliced

sugar, according to taste

It is important to heat mulled wine to a maximum of 80 °C. For that purpose a roast thermometer can help, because in the cold it is hard to estimate the temperature inside the Dutch Oven.

SAFETY NOTE:

Never pour the rum directly from the bottle onto the sugar loaf, as the bottle might explode in your hands. Always use a ladle to pour rum onto the sugar. Have a 10 litre bucket of cold water at hand to immerse the ladle each time before pouring new rum, to cool it down and extinguish the flames. For safety reasons, always have a powder fire extinguisher or fire blanket nearby, because: "It's better to have and not to need than to need and not to have!" An important accessory are Petromax Aramid Pro 300 Gloves, as the fire tongs become hot and have to be removed before getting to the punch.

FEUERZANGENBOWLE
(RED WINE PUNCH)

Especially in the cold months, with the sun setting early, the flames of a Feuerzangenbowle are an impressive sight. Alcohol burns with an almost invisible, blue flame, so for a Feuerzangenbowle it should be as dark as possible.

A proven recipe for a Dutch Oven ft9 consists of five litres of red wine, one litre of orange juice with pulp, a sugar loaf and half a bottle of rum (54%).

Heat up the red wine and the orange juice in a Dutch Oven suspended on a Tripod. Make sure that the fluid is not boiling. Briefly remove the pot from the fire to put the fire tongs for the sugar loaf into place. Put the sugar loaf inside and pour rum on top to let it fully soak and prevent the rum from dripping immediately into the wine. Now, you can ignite the loaf and add rum with a ladle several times while the loaf is burning down.

10 REASONS
FOR PETROMAX CAST IRON

 High-Quality Raw Materials

 Skillet Included

 Fine-Pored Surface

 Seasoned Finish

 Even Material Thickness

 Stable Suspension

 Low Rate of Casting Defects per cm²

 German Engineering

 Clean Post-Production

 Comprehensive Customer Service

www.petromax.de

 Petromax